# DEEPER S[...]
# OF HUMAN [...]

in the Light of the Gospel
of St. Matthew

RUDOLF STEINER

*Three lectures given in Berlin*
*1, 9 and 23 November 1909*

**RUDOLF STEINER PRESS, LONDON**
**ANTHROPOSOPHIC PRESS Inc.**
**NEW YORK**

First Published 1935
Revised edition 1957
Reprinted 1985

*Translation by D. S. Osmond and A. P. Shepherd,
from shorthand reports unrevised by the lecturer.
Published by permission of the Rudolf Steiner-
Nachlassverwaltung, Dornach, Switzerland*

*Cover design by Barbara Manteuffel*

ISBN 0 85440 610 7
ISBN 0 88010 132 6

Printed by Billing & Sons Limited, Worcester

In his autobiography, (chapters 35 and 36), Rudolf Steiner speaks as follows concerning the character of this privately printed matter:

"The contents of this printed matter were intended as oral communications and not for print . . .

"Nothing has ever been said that was not the purest result of Anthroposophy as it developed . . . Whoever reads this privately printed matter can take it in the fullest sense as that which Anthroposophy has to say. Therefore it was possible, and moreover without misgivings . . . to depart from the accepted custom of circulating these publications only among the membership. But it will have to be remembered that faulty passages occur in the transcripts, which I myself did not revise.

"The right to form a judgment on the content of such privately printed matter can be admitted only in the case of one who has acquired the requisite preliminary knowledge. And in respect of all these publications, this is, at the very least, the knowledge of man and of the cosmos in so far as it is presented in Anthroposophy, and of what is to be found as 'anthroposophical history' in the communications from the spiritual world."

# CONTENTS

# FOREWORD

The day will come, Rudolf Steiner once declared, when the whole human race will acclaim the Bible as the greatest book in the world, inasmuch as it will be seen to contain the whole history of the spiritual evolution of mankind.

In the early part of the 19th century, the Bible was almost universally accepted as verbally inspired, but with the widespread advance of science at that time and with the new evolutionary theories of Darwin it was subjected to materialistic scepticism and rationalisation. In the latter part of the nineteenth century it had to meet a new line of criticism in the light of comparative literary and historical knowledge. This in many ways silenced some of the crude earlier attacks. At the turn of the century a wave of archaeological discovery thrust farther back the beginnings of human civilisation and shed new light on the historical basis of the Scripture story. This was followed in the 'twenties, by the new German form-criticism, and later by Maurice Nicoll's treatment of the New Testament claiming to reveal the symbolic character of the text, concealing beneath it a mystical and esoteric meaning.

But also at the turn of the century, in the midst of this stream of Biblical criticism, Rudolf Steiner, unrecognised, indeed almost unnoticed, by the critics, made an entirely different approach to the Bible, in the light of his own spiritual perception and the great principle of human evolution he had thereby discovered. This was no mystical interpretation of the Biblical text, but an application to it of his spiritual understanding of evolution. Thereby light is thrown, not only on the meaning and structure of the whole Bible, but also on incidents and passages, some of them incomprehensible, some seemingly trivial, which can now be seen to fit into the whole pattern of this spiritual background.

Particularly is this so in Rudolf Steiner's treatment of the Gospels. On each Gospel he gave a special course of lectures—two courses on the Gospel of St. John—not as any sort of continuous commentary, but revealing the relation of the Gospels to one another and to the spiritual pattern of which they form an integral part.

These three lectures on St. Matthew's Gospel provide an invaluable introduction to this whole series of Gospel lectures, setting out explicitly their spiritual inter-relationship, and indicating some of the deep principles governing them. The reader may not find himself able at once to accept or understand some of the textual interpretations, but the main lines of the argument and their corroboration in the Biblical text are so convincing, that it is impossible to doubt that here we have an as yet unexplored avenue of discovery, that will lead to the heart of the deepest secrets of Biblical revelation and to a truer understanding of human evolution.

# I

Introductory lectures have already been given on the Gospels of St. John and of St. Luke.[1] The impression they endeavoured to convey can best be described by saying that all through they took the view that the Being of Christ-Jesus—as far as human understanding in our present time is capable of conceiving Him—is so great, so all-embracing, so mighty, that there can be no one-sided presentation of *who* Christ-Jesus was and of His significance for the spirit and soul of every single human being. To attempt anything of the kind would seem presumptuous in the presence of the greatest of all world-problems. Reverence, veneration—these are the appropriate words to express the mood pervading our studies. This reverence expresses itself in the feeling that, when confronting the greatest problem of life, one should try not to place too high a value upon human powers of comprehension, nor even upon the knowledge imparted by a spiritual science able to penetrate into the very highest realms; one should not imagine that human words can ever be capable of describing more than a single aspect of this great, overwhelming problem.

All the lectures given on the Gospel of St. John during the last three years centred around the words contained in that Gospel: " *I am the Light of the world.*" The aim of the lectures was to make this saying comprehensible, and they will have fulfilled their purpose if they bring a gradual understanding of these words, until they become one's own,—or perhaps only an intuition as to their meaning as they stand in the Gospel of St. John.

When, however, you see a light shining, have you, simply by gazing at it or even by discovering something of its nature and properties, understood *what* it is that is shining there? Have you acquired any real knowledge of the sun, simply through perceiving its manifested light? One must realise that it is one thing to perceive the radiance, and quite another to *understand* the light that is working within that radiance. Because the Being of Whom we are speaking can say of Himself: " I am the Light of the world ", it behoves us to grasp the meaning of this saying; but even then we have understood of that Being no more than the particular manifestation of His nature that is expressed in the words: " I am the Light of the world." Everything contained in the lectures on the Gospel of St. John was necessary in order to show that that Being, Who embraces in Himself all cosmic wisdom, is verily the Light of the world. But this Being Himself is infinitely greater than anything that could be conveyed in the lectures on the Gospel of St. John. If anyone were to believe that those lectures had enabled him to understand Christ-Jesus fully and completely, he would be labouring under the erroneous idea that a single manifestation which he dimly divines enables him to understand the whole radiant Being.

10

A different aspect was presented in the lectures on the Gospel of St. Luke. If our studies of the Gospel of St. John might be regarded as a means for helping us to understand the words, " I am the Light of the world ", the lectures on the Gospel of St. Luke—provided they have been grasped with sufficient depth—may be conceived as an exegesis on the words: " *Father, forgive them; for they know not what they do* ", or: " *Father, into thy hands I commend my spirit.*" Here Christ-Jesus is seen, not only as the Light of the world, but as the Being Who makes the offering of supreme self-surrender; the Being Who is all-comprising without losing His own identity; Who in that He is capable of the uttermost sacrifice, of the greatest imaginable self-surrender, is the very fount of Compassion and Love; Whose warmth streams through the life of men and of the earth now and in all ages of time to come. In everything that these words can express, a second aspect of the Being whom we call Christ-Jesus is presented.

In these two Gospels, therefore, this Being has been depicted as the One Who in His compassion can make the supreme sacrifice, and Who shines over all human existence through the power of His light. Light and Love made manifest in the Being of Christ-Jesus—these are the aspects that have been described. And those who have grasped the full compass of our studies of the Gospels of St. John and St. Luke will be able to gather some idea of what in Christ-Jesus was " Light " and what in Him was " Love and Compassion."

11

We have tried, then, to understand two attributes of Christ-Jesus in their universal significance. The meaning of what was said of Christ as the spirit-Light of the world streaming into all things, living and weaving within them as primordial, eternal wisdom, is reflected back to us from the Gospel of St. John. There is no wisdom accessible to man that is not in some way contained in this Gospel. All the wisdom of the universe is there, for he who contemplates this eternal wisdom in Christ-Jesus sees it, not only as it has worked in the remote past, but as it will work in the far distant future. In contemplating this Gospel, therefore, we hover, like the eagle, in heights far above the level of human existence. In glimpsing the sublime Ideas which bring the Gospel of St. John into the range of our understanding, we are carried on the wings of transcendent, transforming Ideas, above all occurrences in the life of the individual human soul. These all-embracing, eternal Ideas are the concern of that Divine Wisdom which flows to us as we steep ourselves in this Gospel. What streams from it seems itself to be circling, like the eagle, in heights high above every happening in the daily, hourly, and momentary destiny of men.

Let us now descend from these heights, and contemplate individual human life from hour to hour, from day to day, from year to year, from century to century, from millennium to millennium, observing especially the forces expressed in what we call human love. We can perceive love surging and weaving in the living hearts and souls of men through the ages. On the one side we see how this love gives rise to deeds of supreme heroism in the life of mankind, how the greatest sacrifices spring from love for some being or cause; but we also see that, although supreme accomplishments are born of this love in human hearts, it is at the same time like a two-edged sword. For example, a mother loves her child inwardly, deeply; the child commits some misdeed, but so intense is the mother's love that she cannot bring herself to punish. A second misdeed occurs, and again the depth of the mother's love keeps her from punishing the child . . . and so it goes on. The child grows up, becomes a life-long good-for-nothing, a disturber of the peace. In speaking of matters as grave as this it is not good to take contemporary examples, so I will speak of something that happened a long time ago. In the first half of the nineteenth century there was a mother who loved her child with the very deepest intensity. Let it be emphasised that love in itself cannot be too highly valued, for whatever the circumstances, love remains one of the very highest human attri-butes.—But so great was the mother's love that she could not bring herself to punish the child for having committed a petty theft in the home. A second theft was again left unpunished, and finally the child became a notorious poisoner. Such was the outcome of the *lack of wisdom*, in the mother's love. If love is pervaded by wisdom, it is capable of deeds of untold greatness. The significance of the Love that streamed into the world from Golgotha lies precisely in the fact that it was united, in a single

Being, with the Light of the world, with true Wisdom. It is therefore when we contemplate these two qualities as manifested in Christ-Jesus, that we realise that Love is the crowning glory of the world, but also that Love and Wisdom belong in the deepest sense together.

What have we actually understood from our studies of the Gospels of St. John and St. Luke? We have understood nothing beyond those attributes of Christ-Jesus which we may call the universal Light of Wisdom and the universal Warmth of Love, both of which flowed in Him as in no other Being, and which can never be wholly within the reach of our human comprehension. Whereas in connection with the Gospel of St. John we may speak of great, transcendental Ideas sweeping like eagles in heights far above the heads of men, in the Gospel of St. Luke we find that which speaks at every moment to each individual human heart. The significance of St. Luke's Gospel is that it fills us with a warmth that is the outward expression of love, with understanding for the love that is ready to make the supreme sacrifice, which has no other desire than to surrender its very self.

A pictorial presentation of the mood and feeling arising from a right approach to the Gospel of St. Luke is to be found in portrayals of the Mithras bull being driven to the sacrifice, bearing on its back the figure of a man. Seen from below it is an earthly happening; but above the moving figures cosmic events hover. The man thrusts his knife into the body of the sacrificial bull, whose life-

14

blood is offered up in order that man may conquer what has to be overcome. Contemplation of the sacrificial animal carrying the man, for whose sake it must be sacrificed in order that, as man, he may be able to advance along his path of life, provides the right basis of feeling for study of the Gospel of St. Luke. Those who know what the sacrificial bull, as the expression of inwardly deepened love, has betokened for men through all the ages, understand something of the qualities of love described in the Gospel of St. Luke. This Gospel, then, depicts a second attribute of Christ-Jesus.

But does knowledge of two attributes or qualities of a Being justify the claim to have understood the whole nature of that Being? It has been necessary to speak of these two attributes because in Christ-Jesus the greatest of all riddles stands before us. But no one should maintain that study of two such attributes yields anything like a true or complete picture of the nature of this Being. In describing these two attributes of Christ-Jesus, nothing that can bring even a glimmering understanding of their infinite significance has been left unsaid. But our reverence and awe for this Being is too great ever to allow us to imagine that thereby we have already grasped His other attributes.

It would be possible to speak of a third attribute, but as it involves matters which have not yet formed part of our studies, a general indication of it is all that can here be given. I may put it in this way. The Christ presented in the Gospel of St. John is, in Himself, a Being of the utmost sublimity, but in

His works He draws upon the powers pertaining to the realm of the wisdom-filled *Cherubim*. It is for this reason that, in describing the Christ of St. John's Gospel, the dominating feeling will be that evoked by the picture of the eagle-soaring Cherubim. In the Gospel of St. Luke, however, the keynote of the picture is the warmth-bringing fire of love springing from the heart of Christ. This indicates that in what Christ signified to the world in this Gospel, He worked at those sublime heights which are the realm of the *Seraphim*. The fiery love of the Seraphim streams through the universe, and is conveyed to our earth through Christ-Jesus. But there is a third aspect to be considered, namely, what Christ-Jesus signified for the earthly world in that He was not alone the Light of Wisdom, not alone the Warmth of Love, not alone the channel for the Cherubim and Seraphim within earth-existence, but with His whole Power 'was' and 'is' within this earth-existence, inasmuch as He worked in the realm of the *Thrones*, the realm whence all Strength and Power flow into the world, to the end that Wisdom and Love may be led to fulfilment. Seraphim, Cherubim, Thrones: these are the three highest Spiritual Hierarchies. The Seraphim with their Love lead us into the depths of the human heart, the Cherubim with their Wisdom upwards to the heights of the *eagle*. Wisdom shines down upon us from those heights while self-surrendering Love is symbolised in the sacrificial *bull*. But Strength pulsing through the world, Strength which makes all things possible of fulfilment, Strength which is the creative power surging

16

through the world, for these, in all systems of symbolism, the token is the *lion*. The Strength infused into our earth through Christ-Jesus, the Strength which orders and directs all things and which, when it is unfolded, signifies supreme Power —that is what is described in the Gospel of St. Mark as a third attribute of Christ-Jesus. In connection with the Gospel of St. John we speak of Christ as the sublime Sun-Being, as the *Light* of the Earth-Sun in the spiritual sense; in connection with the Gospel of St. Luke we speak of the warmth of the *Love* streaming from Christ; in connection with the Gospel of St. Mark we shall speak of the *Power* of the Earth-Sun in the spiritual sense. Study of the Gospel of St. Mark will give us a picture of the forces present in the earth, of the working and weaving of earthly forces and powers, both hidden and manifest.[2] If by lifting ourselves to Christ in the sense of St. John's Gospel we can claim to have some faint inkling of the transcendent Ideas which came to the earth as His earthly Thoughts, if we can feel the warmth of His self-giving Love by letting the warmth streaming from St. Luke's Gospel pervade our own hearts,—if thus in St. John's Gospel we can glimpse Christ's *Thinking*, and in St. Luke's Gospel His *Feeling*—then in St. Mark's Gospel we can learn of His *Willing*; we are presented with a picture of the forces by means of which Christ brings Love and Wisdom to actual fulfilment.

If the Gospel of St. Mark had been studied in addition to the Gospels of St. John and St. Luke,

17

a tentative understanding of three attributes of Christ Jesus would be within our reach. We should then have the right to say: " With all reverence we have come nearer to Thee, and we have dimly divined something of Thy Thinking, Thy Feeling, Thy Willing. These three attributes of Thy Being hover above us as supreme prototypes of earthly existence! " We begin our study of an ordinary human being in the same way when we speak of Sentient Soul, Mind-Soul and Spiritual Soul, and study the characteristics and functions of each. Of the ' Spiritual Soul ' of Christ we can say that we acquire an insight into the understanding of it from St. John's Gospel; the ' Mind-Soul ' of Christ becomes comprehensible to us through St. Luke's Gospel; and the ' Sentient Soul ' of Christ, with all its forces of will, through St. Mark's Gospel. When we come to study this last Gospel, light will be shed on the forces of Nature, both manifest and hidden, concentrated in the single Individuality of Christ, and on the essential character of all the forces operating in the world. The Gospel of St. John has deepened our understanding of the Thoughts of this Being, the Gospel of St. Luke our understanding of His Feelings, and because man is not wont to penetrate so deeply into these two realms of the life of soul, studies of the Gospels of St. John and St. Luke are relatively simple in comparison with the picture, presented in the Gospel of St. Mark, of the system and organisation of the hidden forces, both natural and spiritual, operating in the world. All this stands revealed in the Akasha

Chronicle and it will be mirrored before us when we pass on to study the power-filled Gospel of St. Mark. Then we shall begin to discern all that is concentrated in the Being of Christ, and which otherwise is distributed among the whole variety of individual beings in the world. We shall then be able to understand, and perceive in a higher, clearer way, all that we have learnt to know as the fundamental elemental laws and principles behind all kinds of existence. As we grasp the meaning of the Gospel of St. Mark, which contains all the secrets of the Universal Will, then, in all reverence, we draw nearer to Christ-Jesus, the focal point of the Universe, inasmuch as more and more we apprehend His Thinking, His Feeling and His Willing.

When we observe the interplay of human thinking, feeling and willing, we have an approximate picture of the whole man. But in observing a single human being, we cannot help envisaging each of these activities separately. Yet when we bring them together again into a collective whole our observation cannot be anything like exhaustive. We make our task easier by observing each of the three functions separately, but on the other hand, the picture will lose precision when we bring them together again as a united whole. It is for our own advantage, then, that we separate the functions, inasmuch as a collective survey of the whole is beyond our power, but the picture becomes blurred when the attributes are brought together again.— In the same way, if we have acquired from the

Gospels of St. John, St. Luke and St. Mark some conception of the Thinking, Feeling and Willing of Christ-Jesus, we can attempt to harmonise these three attributes into a united whole. The picture will inevitably lose precision and vividness, for no human faculty is capable of unifying what it has made separate and distinct. In Being itself there is unity, not separation; but for us, only at the final stage is it possible to gather the separated attributes into a unity. Although it will be less vivid, we shall at last have a presentation of what Christ-Jesus was as earthly Man.

It is in the Gospel of St. Matthew that the picture is drawn for us of Christ-Jesus as man, of His life as a man during the thirty-three years of His sojourn on earth. The contents of St. Matthew's Gospel present us with a harmonised human portrait. In St. John's Gospel we saw a Divine and Cosmic Man, in St. Luke's Gospel a Being Who is the embodiment of self-giving Love, and in St. Mark's Gospel the cosmic Will operating in a single Individuality. In St. Matthew's Gospel we have the portrait of the Man of Palestine who during the thirty-three years of His life united in His own Being everything we have gathered from our study of the other three Gospels. Yet this picture of Christ-Jesus as a human being, as an earthly man, can be understood only against the background provided by our previous studies. As we saw was the case with the individual human being, so too, in this case, the attributes presented in the other three accounts are here less vividly apparent. But

20

a picture of the *human* personality of Christ-Jesus can be afforded only by study of the Gospel of St. Matthew.

The situation is quite different from that in which we approached the study of St. John's Gospel. Now that the study of two Gospels lies behind us, we can perceive how they are inwardly related to each other and that we can only obtain a complete picture of Christ-Jesus if, with a similar approach, we consider the Man Who lived upon the earth as Christ-Jesus. From St. John's Gospel we have a picture of the Divine Man, from St. Luke's Gospel a picture of the Being Who unites in Himself all the streams which came to expression in Zoroastrianism, and also in Buddhism with its teaching of compassion and love. All this from the past came before us when we studied the Gospel of St. Luke. Study of the Gospel of St. Matthew will give us, first and foremost, an intimate and faithful picture of a Being who is the offspring of His own people the ancient Hebrew race. And we shall come to realise why the blood of this people had to be prepared in a definite way in order to provide for mankind the blood of Christ-Jesus. The study of St. Matthew's Gospel will give us a picture not only of the essential character of Hebraic antiquity, but also of the mission of this people for the whole world, of the birth of the new era, of the birth of Christianity out of the ancient Hebrew world. What Christ-Jesus was and is as Man, and the secrets of human history and human evolution—these are contained in the Gospel of St. Matthew.

21

Thus, through the Gospel of St. John we glimpse the Ideas of the Divine Sophia, through the Gospel of St. Luke the mysteries of supreme, self-giving Love, through the Gospel of St. Mark the forces and powers of the earth and the cosmos, and through the Gospel of St. Matthew we learn to understand human life, human history, human destiny.

If out of the seven years of the existence of our movement, four years had been devoted to acquainting ourselves with the principles and guiding-lines of spiritual science, and three to deepening our understanding of them as a light that must be shed on the many diverse domains of life, we might now have passed on to the study of St. Mark's Gospel, and the whole edifice could have been crowned by the study of Christ-Jesus as presented in St. Matthew's Gospel. But as human life has its limitations and this level has not been reached— at any rate in the case of everyone in the movement —it is not possible, without evoking misconceptions, to proceed at once to the study of St. Mark's Gospel. It would denote complete misunderstanding of the Being of Christ to believe that any knowledge of His nature could be derived from St. John's Gospel or St. Luke's Gospel alone, or from a one-sided application of all that is revealed in St. Mark's Gospel. The misunderstandings would be even greater than they have been already.

In view of all this we must choose the other path and pass on, as best we may, to the study of St. Matthew's Gospel. Although this means that for the present we must forego the profundities of St.

Mark's Gospel, it will prevent any repetition of the belief that by describing a single attribute, a picture is given of the whole Being, and thereby it will be possible to avoid wrong conclusions.

We shall now turn our minds to Christ-Jesus as the offspring of the ancient Hebrew people, and to the birth of Christianity in Palestine. Our studies will be based on the Gospel of St. Matthew and it will then be easier to proceed to what we shall have to say about the Gospel of St. Mark.

## II

Reference was made in the last lecture to our proposed study of the Gospels and we explained why we had decided to begin with certain aspects of St. Matthew's Gospel. In the first place it is in this Gospel that the most human side of Christ-Jesus is presented. Secondly, there is given in it a complete survey of events which show how the coming of Christ-Jesus is related to human history. This is a direct indication that this greatest of all phenomena on earth represents the culmination of actual historical events, and it is therefore natural to assume that this particular Gospel brings us face to face with the deeper secrets of the evolution of humanity.

Once again I must emphasise that the things of which we shall now be speaking call for accurate treatment, and that great harm can easily be done to the cause of Spiritual Science by giving to the general public any incomplete or one-sided picture of matters connected with these secrets. All communications should be made with great caution; nor is it too much to expect everyone to have the patience to refrain from attempting to present to himself a complete picture of Christ-Jesus until he has become acquainted with the four aspects revealed by the four Gospels.

In the Gospel of St. Luke we are shown how the

24

two great pre-Christian streams of spiritual life—
Zoroastrianism and the stream which reached its
pre-Christian culmination in Buddhism—united,
in order to pour themselves into the great Christian
stream of spiritual life on the earth. The Gospel
of St. Matthew is concerned primarily, with a quite
different theme, namely, to show how and in what
respects the physical entity in which the Zarathustra-
Individuality incarnated springs from the ancient
Hebrew people. It attempts to set out the part
played by the ancient Hebrew people in the whole
evolutionary process of mankind. It might easily
be imagined that if the Zarathustra-Individuality
incarnated in Jesus of Bethlehem, it was simply a
matter of the body being born from the Hebrew
people, and that this implies nothing more than that
Zarathustra was reborn in a body of Hebrew stock.
Such a conception would give rise to an entirely
misleading picture of the truth.

We must realise more and more clearly the fact
that an Individuality as great as Zarathustra uses
the body as an *instrument*. Even if a Being were
to come down to the earth out of the highest, even
the very highest, divine worlds, and were to incarnate
in an unsuitable physical organism, such a Being
could make use of that body only to the extent to
which it was actually capable of being an instrument.
It is for this reason that the mistaken line of thought
just referred to would readily lead to misconceptions.
That man's bodily organism is the temple of the
soul has long ceased to be properly understood.
We must always remember what has so often been

emphasised among us, namely, that the human Ego dwells within three sheaths, each one of which is more ancient than the Ego itself. The Ego is a being of Earth, the youngest of the members of man's nature. The astral body had its beginning on the Old Moon, the etheric or life-body on the Old Sun, the physical body on Old Saturn.[3] This means that the physical body is the most highly perfected, having four stages of planetary evolution behind it. The physical body has been developed through aeon after aeon until it has become what it is to-day—this perfect instrument in which the human Ego can so unfold that man can be enabled gradually to rise again to the heights of the spirit. If the physical body were as undeveloped as the astral body and the Ego, no evolution on the earth would be possible for man.

If you realise the full significance of this, the thought of Zarathustra being born from the Hebrew people can no longer be clouded by any mistaken feeling. The constitution of the ancient Hebrew people had to be just what it was, if it was to provide the body for a being as great as Zarathustra. If we bear in mind that ever since the time when he had been the Teacher of the ancient Persian people, this great being had been developing to ever higher stages, we shall understand that for him a bodily instrument had to be provided from a racial stock whose greatness was commensurate with that of his own being.

An instrument had to be created, fit for Zarathustra. Through all the evolutionary periods of

Saturn, Sun, Moon and Earth, have the gods worked at the development of the human physical body. From this we may rightly infer that the more intimate preparation of one particular human body must necessarily have entailed great divine-spiritual labour, in order to produce a human body in the specially constituted form which was to be used at that time by Zarathustra.

To make this possible, the whole history of the ancient Hebrew people had to take the course it did. The Akasha Chronicle reveals that what is set down in the Old Testament conforms entirely with the historical facts. Everything that happened to the ancient Hebrew people had to be directed in such a way that it culminated in the single personality of Jesus of Bethlehem. But to achieve this, very special measures were essential.—It was necessary that from the whole of Post-Atlantean civilisation, faculties of the highest quality should be extracted, which would enable mankind to develop powers *in place of the old clairvoyant gifts*. It was the Hebrew people which was chosen for this task, to the end that it might provide a bodily constitution which, right into the most delicate vessels of the brain, was so organised that what we call *knowledge of the world* might evolve, free from the influences of the old clairvoyance.—This was to be the mission of the ancient Hebrew people. And in Abraham, the progenitor of this people, such an Individuality was chosen, that out of his bodily constitution, a suitable instrument might be fashioned for the development of reasoned thinking.[4]

All previous thinking of any significance was still subject to the influences of the old clairvoyance. But now a personality was chosen because he possessed the brain most capable of withstanding the inrush and coercion of clairvoyant Imaginations and Intuitions, and was destined to acquire know-of the things of the world purely by the process of reason. This required a specially constituted brain, and the personality chosen because he possessed such a brain, was Abram, or Abraham.

That the path of Abraham's journeyings led westwards from beyond the river Euphrates right up to Canaan, also tallies with what the Akasha Chronicle reveals. Abraham went forth, as the Bible tells us, from Ur in Chaldea. Whereas the aftermath of the ancient, shadowy clairvoyance was still in active operation in Egyptian, as well as in Chaldean-Babylonian civilisation, there was chosen from among the Chaldeans an individual who no longer worked by means of these faculties, but *by observing the phenomena of the external world*. This was to be the introduction of that form of culture whose fruits are to this very day implicit in the whole of the cultural life and civilisation of the West. Constructive reasoning and mathematical logic were both introduced through Abraham. Even until far into the Middle Ages he was regarded in a certain sense as the founder of arithmetic. The fundamental trend and character of his thinking led to observation of the world according to the relationships of *measure* and *number*.*

* See Appendix I, p. 72

28

A personality so constituted was able, by his very nature, to enter into living relationship with that Divinity who was to reveal himself through the medium of external phenomena. All other Divinities, with the exception of Jahve or Jehovah, proclaimed themselves in the inmost depths of the human soul, and to acquire any knowledge of them man had to awaken in his soul the faculties of Imagination, Inspiration and Intuition. The men of ancient India gazed at the rising sun, at the different kingdoms of the earth, at the processes manifesting in air and ocean, but regarded all this as a great Illusion, as " Maya ", in which they would have found nothing of a divine nature, had they not first acquired knowledge of the divine through inner Imagination, and then, afterwards, had proceeded to relate this knowledge to the phenomena of the external world. It must be realised that even Zarathustra could not have taught as he did of the mighty Sun-Being had not Ahura Mazdao in his glory been *inwardly* revealed to him. This is especially apparent in the case of the Egyptian divinities, who were first experienced in the inmost depths of the soul and only afterwards related to the things of the external world. All that applies to the Divinities of pre-Hebraic times must be understood in this way.

Jahve, however, is the Divine Being who gazes down upon men from *outside*, who comes to men from outside, manifesting Himself in wind and weather. When man penetrates to the relationships of number, measure and weight inhering in the things of the visible world, he draws near to the God Jahve.—In earlier times the process was reversed. Brahma was recognised, first, in the inmost depths of the soul and only from that experience did man find his way into the outer world. Jahve is recognised first in the outer world and only afterwards can his reality also be confirmed in man's inmost being. This is the spiritual aspect of what is called in the Bible: Jahve's covenant with Abraham. Abraham was a man who possessed the faculty to grasp and comprehend the nature of Jahve. Abraham's bodily constitution was such that he could recognise Jahve or Jehovah as the God who lives and moves in the outer phenomena of the universe.

It was now a matter of deriving from the particular faculties possessed by the individual man Abraham, the mission of a whole people. Abraham's spiritual constitution had to be transmitted to others. But this spiritual constitution is bound up with the physical instrument; whatever is to be brought to outward expression depends upon the physical body being organised in a definite and specific way. In the ancient religions, built up as they were on the foundation of shadowy clairvoyance, the particular formation of the various parts of the brain was not of such essential importance. Understanding of *Jehovah*, however, was fundamentally bound up with the constitution of the physical brain. Only by way of physical heredity, within a people linked by *blood-relationship*, could such faculties and qualities be transmitted.

Very special measures were necessary for the achievement of this end. Abraham must have descendants who would carry to further stages of development that unique physical organism which until then had been the work of the gods and which had come to its most perfect expression in Abraham. The elaboration of the physical, bodily constitution was now to be taken in hand by man independently and that which for long ages had been the work of the gods be led by man to further stages. That this process must extend over many generations is self-evident. A brain capable of understanding Jahve had to be preserved through physical heredity. Jahve's covenant with Abraham had also to pass on to his descendants. This, however, called for the uttermost devotion to Jahve on the part of Abraham; for it is possible to develop a particular organism to further stages only if it is used in conformity with the purpose for which it was originally created. If, with a certain aim in view, it is desirable that the hands, for example, shall be made particularly skilful, this can only be achieved by developing them in accordance with their own inherent character. If the physical qualities of the brain had to be developed to the point where comprehension of Jahve was possible, then devotion to and understanding of Jahve must have reached in Abraham the highest conceivable degree of intensity.

That was exactly what happened, as the Bible relates. Self-sacrifice is supreme when a man offers up all that the future holds in store for his own self. Abraham is called upon to sacrifice his son Isaac

31

to Jahve. Therewith he would have sacrificed the whole Hebrew people, all that he himself was, and all that had to be brought, through him, into the world. Abraham was the very first human being who truly understood Jahve, in that he knew that if he desired to give proof of the fulness of his devotion, he must surrender himself utterly to Jahve. Through offering his only son, however, Abraham renounced the propagation of his line in the world. But so complete was his devotion that with full resolve, he offered up Isaac.

Then Isaac was restored to him. What does this signify? It signifies something of supreme importance. Abraham receives Isaac back at the hand of Jahve. This brings to Abraham the realisation that the mission that is his by virtue of his own Individuality he will not pass on to posterity through his own deed, but he is to receive it in the person of his son as a gift of Jahve.[5] Anyone who ponders this deeply will realise that here we have a fact of cosmic significance, whereby immeasurable light is shed upon the secrets of the historical evolution of humanity.

Now let us consider how events proceed.— Through Abraham's devotion to Jahve was made possible the right development of that which had hitherto been the work of the gods, namely the physical nature of humanity which had come into being out of the universe. As we know, the physical bodily constitution of man on the earth is connected, according to number, measure and weight, with all the laws governing the world of the stars. Out of the world of the stars man is born; in his very being he embodies the laws of that world. These laws had, as it were, to be inscribed into the blood flowing down from Abraham through the generations of the ancient Hebrew people. In this people everything must be so regulated as to ensure the continuance of the stream of ordered law which, flowing from the universe, has organised the human physical body according to the principles of number, measure and weight prevailing in the constellations. Again this is indicated in an utterance in the Bible, which is completely mistranslated. " I will make thy seed as the stars of heaven."[6] The meaning of the words is in no wise that God will make the Israelites *as numerous* as the stars of heaven, but that the way in which this people multiply and spread on the earth shall be governed by the laws and number-relationships prevailing in the ordering of the stars in heaven. The propagation of the Hebrew people was to be regulated in accordance with the number-harmonies of the stars.

We can see how this comes to pass. Isaac has two sons, Jacob and Esau. We see how all that was carried by the blood through the generations develops,—the blood of the line of Esau having been cut out and the main stream separated from it. Again, Jacob has twelve sons, corresponding to the twelve signs of the Zodiac through which the sun passes in the heavens, thus fulfilling the inner principle of the starry laws. Thus the number and measure prevailing in the heavens are factually portrayed to us in the life and descent, through their generations, of the Hebrew people.

33

Again, Abraham was ready to sacrifice his son Isaac, and thereby he received back his whole mission at the hand of Jahve. A ram or lamb is sacrificed in place of Isaac. This signifies something of the greatest profundity. The human corporality which was to propagate itself through the generations and which possessed the faculties necessary for comprehending the world according to number and measure, by mathematical logic—this human corporality was to be preserved intact and received back as the gift of Jahve. But in order that the intrinsic nature of this bodily constitution should remain pure and unalloyed, it was necessary that all old, shadowy clairvoyance, all Imaginations and Intuitions, all inflowing revelations such as had poured into the other ancient religions, including those of Chaldea and Egypt, should be renounced. Every gift from the spiritual world must be renounced. The last gift from the spiritual world, the one gift remaining after all the others have dimmed, is denoted in mystical symbolism by the *Ram*. The two horns of the ram symbolise the sacrifice of the two-petalled lotus-flower.[7] The last clairvoyant gift is sacrificed, the others having already been laid aside in earlier times. In order that this bodily constitution might be preserved in Isaac, the last clairvoyant gift, the gift of the ram, the two-petalled lotus-flower is sacrificed.

As the mission of the Hebrew people progresses, these Abrahamitic faculties are transmitted from generation to generation. Whenever the old clairvoyance reappears as an atavistic element, whenever

34

any individual sees once more into the spiritual world, the immediate reaction is that he is cast out from his people, he is not tolerated within the community. Antipathy against this gift of the ram expresses itself in direct hostility. This is exemplified in the enmity meted out to Joseph. Prophetic illuminations from the spiritual world come to Joseph in his dreams. Quite naturally he is thrust out from his people, because the gift he possesses is not in keeping with their mission, because a heritage of ancient clairvoyance appears again in him. Such is the profound meaning of the story here narrated.

On the other hand we see that something essential for the development of the Hebrew people and the fulfilment of their mission is in turn provided through Joseph, that is, through the very personality in whom was preserved a heritage which the Hebrew people could only regard as belonging to the age *before* Abraham. In a certain sense the gate to the world, from which, through the old shadowy clairvoyance, the ancient Indian and Persian civilisations had received their religions, was closed against the Hebrew people. That gate being closed, they now looked out into the world, classified it according to measure and number, and in its all-embracing unity they beheld Jahve or Jehovah. One thing more they knew, and that was that the visible world they beheld around them and which found its unity as being entirely the creation of Jehovah, was of the same nature as the *Egohood* of mankind.

35

But within this race-community, no Imaginations, no inner, personal experiences arose regarding these things. At *that* time this people themselves had no such inner experiences. Therefore it was necessary that they should be taught from outside, that they should learn from a people who still had these experiences. And so Joseph forms the link between the ancient Hebrew people and the Egyptians, the people from whom could be learnt those things of which the ancient Hebrews themselves had no longer actual experience. The whole picture which a man to-day is able to form out of his own inner experiences, the knowledge and experience derived from the outer world and from inner imagination—this had to be acquired at that time by contacting a people in whom such experiences still abounded—the Egyptian people. Harmony had to be established between inner faculties of this nature and what was acquired by the ancient Hebrews through mathematical logic and reasoning. But contact with the Egyptian people could be initiated only by a personality who himself possessed in some measure this faculty of Imagination. Joseph was the appropriate link because he still possessed this faculty.

There were two reasons why he could be of help to the Egyptians.—Firstly, he was gifted with the old clairvoyance belonging to the age before Abraham, and this enabled him to understand and interpret what the ancient Egyptians obtained through their clairvoyance. But what the Egyptian people did not possess was the faculty of mathematical logic—that is to say, they were not able to apply their powers of Imagination to physical life. Hence Pharaoh was incapable of effective action when unprecedented events befell. Imaginations were accessible, but when unprecedented factors occurred, to weigh up and assess intelligently what steps were necessary and to take appropriate measures, required a different faculty, which the Egyptians did not possess. Because Joseph possessed this faculty he was able to give the right counsels at the Egyptian court and so became the appropriate personality to form the link between the Hebrew people and the Egyptians. In this way, through him the Jahve-doctrine—which until then might be described as a synthesis of outer reality in the form of a mathematical world-picture—received colour and substance from the inner faculty of Imagination possessed by the Egyptians.

The actual harmonising and unification of the ancient Egyptian clairvoyant experiences with the Hebrew experience of the outer world-order was effected by Moses.[8] Once this had been achieved, the Hebrew people could be led back again and proceed to work out, in their own way and in accordance with their own nature, what had been acquired in Egypt—though not in the form of actual experiences. For it was essential, as we have seen, that their particular gift should not be mingled with that of any other people, that the quality inherent in their own blood should remain pure and unadulterated. At the same time, the fruits of the spiritual experience of the ancient world had also to be preserved;

37

and so the ancient heritage which still survived in the wisdom of the Egyptians was inculcated, through Moses, into the Hebrew people with their faculties of mathematical logic. Then this people had again to be extricated from that relationship, for they were destined to inherit that *new* faculty which could operate *only* through the descendants of Abraham.

It was because in the course of their history the blood of this people was regulated in strict accordance with its initial principles, because they developed, as they did, in this direction, through their successive generations, that it became possible at a certain definite point of time that there should issue from their stock the body of the Jesus-child,* into which the personality of Zarathustra could incarnate. But in order to achieve this goal the ancient Hebrew people had to grow strong and powerful.

If in the light of St. Matthew's Gospel we study the times of the Judges and Kings and follow the destinies of the ancient Hebrews, we shall see that even the circumstances which seem to indicate that this people is going astray, were for a definite purpose. Above all was it necessary that the misfortune of being led into captivity in Babylon should befall them. We shall see that their racial qualities had developed to the point when it was necessary that they should be brought into contact with the other side of the ancient tradition, as it existed in Babylon. The Hebrew people had reached sufficient maturity to be united once again with faculties

* See Appendix II, p. 75

38

that had been abandoned.—That is one side of the picture.

The other side is that at the very time when the Hebrew people were brought into contact with the Babylonians a great Teacher from the East was working there, with the result that it was possible for some of the best among the Hebrews to receive the illumination of his teaching. This was the time when Zarathustra—in the person of Nazarathos or Zaratas—was teaching in the regions whither the Hebrews were led. Some of the greatest of the Prophets came under his influence. In this way it became possible to inculcate into the Hebrew people what was needed when their blood had already reached a certain stage of development, and influences from outside were required.

We shall not go very far wrong if we compare this whole racial evolution with the gradual growth of the individual human being. When a child is born, it remains until its seventh year in the bodily care of the parents. During this period, the influences that affect it are mainly at the physical level. Then begins the phase inaugurated by the birth—in a real sense—of the etheric body. Development is based on the elaboration of the memory, on which depends the healthy growth of all the possibilities of the etheric body. The beginning of the third period may be described by saying that the human being now enters into relation with the external world through his astral body, at which stage he must acquire the faculty of individual judgment.—The ancient Hebrew people passed

39

through these phases of development in a special way. The first period—from Abraham to the time of the early Kings—may be compared with the first period of the life of the individual human being up to the seventh year. Everything that then happened was for the purpose of establishing in them the particular qualities of their blood. Abraham's journeyings, the development of the twelve tribes, the introduction of the Mosaic laws, the perils in the desert—all these happenings can be compared with what flows into the human being on the physical plane during the first seven years of life. Then comes the second period: the inner consolidation of the race, the rulership of the Kings up to the time of the captivity in Babylon.—Then follows the third stage, when the influence of Chaldean wisdom is brought to bear upon the Hebrews. And the Leader, through whom at that time—600 to 550 B.C.—was released the inflow of this oriental influence into the Hebrew people, was none other than the Individuality who in ancient Persia had been Zarathustra. Thus already at the time of the Babylonian captivity Zarathustra was preparing the way that would lead to the finding of a suitable bodily organism. So down the generations from Abraham onwards there developed more and more the requisite conditions for the birth of the bodily organism in which Zarathustra could reincarnate.

The threefold grouping indicated in the genealogy at the beginning of St. Matthew's Gospel gives a wonderfully faithful picture of this evolutionary

process. There are three times 14 generations.—
" From Abraham to David, 14 generations; from
David to the time of the Babylonian captivity,
14 generations; from the Babylonian capitivity to
Christ-Jesus, 14 generations." (St. Matthew I. 17).
There are three times 14, that is, 42 generations.
This is an indication that the bodily constitution
of Jesus is an embodiment of the purest extract of
all that had been in preparation from Abraham down-
wards, through all the vicissitudes and destinies
undergone by the ancient Hebrew people. Finally
a human being must appear, who in his soul and
in his deeds will express all the qualities matured
in the race, in his individual personality. The
whole development of the Hebrew people from the
time of Abraham was to reach its culmination in a
single man—in the Jesus of St. Matthew's Gospel.

Such a culmination can be reached only if the
whole course of preceding development is recapitulated in a spiritual way. Zarathustra goes forth—
in a spiritual sense from the Mysteries—from Ur
of the Chaldees, the same region whence Abraham
had been called. It is there that the " Golden
Star " first appears, and then goes forth, followed by
the Magi of the land. What had come to pass
physically through Abraham is now re-enacted
spiritually. The star which the Magi follow moves
in spiritual fashion along the path once travelled
by Abraham. The star taking this path and coming
to rest upon the birthplace is the incarnating
Zarathustra himself. This is the moment when
the Zarathustra-Individuality incarnates in the child

41

Jesus of Bethlehem. The Magi knew that, in following the star, they were following their great Teacher, Zarathustra, on his way to reincarnation.

It is now a matter of perceiving how this path continues and of realising how the purest extract of the whole evolution of the Hebrew people is actually present in the personality of the Jesus described in St. Matthew's Gospel. Firstly, we see that spiritually the sacrificial offering of Isaac is repeated in the offering of gold, frankincense and myrrh brought by the three Magi from the East. We are reminded, too, of other happenings among the ancient Hebrew people. The circumstances associated with the birth of this Jesus-Child are like a reflection of the destinies of the ancient Hebrews. Among them was a Joseph who in his dreams possessed an inherited gift and was able to form the link between the Hebrew and the Egyptian peoples; now again there is a Joseph who has dreams and to whom it is shown in a dream, not only that Jesus will be born, but that he must go with Jesus to Egypt.

The path of Zarathustra—now living in the body of the Jesus-child—continues. Just as he had followed the path taken by Abraham on the physical plane from Ur in Chaldea to Canaan, so he follows it further still, to Egypt. Like the Hebrew people, the Jesus-child is brought back again from Egypt. Thus, in the appearance of the Bethlehem Jesus— only later called the Nazarene—there is a recapitulation of the whole destiny of the ancient Hebrew people up to the return from Egypt to Palestine, the Promised Land. Events in the outer history of the Hebrew people, extending over long, long centuries, are now recapitulated in the destiny of that human being who was Zarathustra incarnated in the body of the Bethlehem Jesus. This—conceived on the vast scale in which it is presented in the Gospel of St. Matthew—is the secret of human history in general. Human history cannot be understood unless it is recognised that in the destiny of every great Individuality charged with a special mission the whole process of development through centuries is recapitulated; that such Individualities represent the essence and extract of what has been achieved in history through long ages. Far, far more than this was, of course, to be embodied in Christ-Jesus, but the bodily constitution had first to be prepared, and this was possible only through the special measures that have been described.

What kind of conditions prevailed at the point of time when the whole history of the Hebrew people was to be recapitulated in the personality of Jesus?—In what way was it a turning-point of history? Let us here review the following facts of the evolutionary process of which for some years now I have been trying to give you a picture.

Humanity proceeded from a primeval stage of evolution when everything that brought human beings together in love was bound up with the blood-tie. Love was determined by this factor, and marriage took place only between human beings very closely related by blood. In those ancient

43

times there was no other kind of love than that which was bound up with blood-relationship. From this 'close marriage' humanity had its beginnings. But intermingling of the particular blood-ties gradually became more general in widely separated territories of the earth. Among all the peoples, however, there is evidence to show that they were taken aback when men and women belonging to one racial stock marry into a different stock, when the transition to 'distant marriage' begins. In all the myths and sagas, in the legend of Gudrun, for example, this is described as an unwonted happening, one that causes astonishment.

Two streams were in operation during this phase of human evolution. In the process where human beings are brought together through ties of blood there was working the Divine-Spiritual principle which strives to unite humanity, to unify all mankind. Working in opposition to this was the Luciferic principle which strives to make every human being independent, to endow the single individual with the greatest possible power. Both these principles must be present in human nature, both forces must take effect in the evolution of humanity.

These two sets of powers, then, were at work in the progressive evolution of humanity: the Divine-Spiritual powers on the one hand, and on the other, the Luciferic powers, spirit-beings who had not completed their evolution on the Old Moon and who wished to prevent men from losing their identity as separate beings, and to make them entirely independent and self-sufficient. These opposing powers were always at work, and as a result, the Ego of man, a product of the earth, was perpetually being torn to this side or to that—towards human love on the one side and towards inner self-sufficiency on the other.

Now at a particular point of time the interworking of these two powers reached a kind of crisis. This crisis, this crucial condition in human affairs set in when, as the result of the deeds of the Roman Empire, widespread intermingling took place among the peoples in many territories of the earth. This was a most crucial moment in the evolution of humanity, the moment when the still undecided question of close or distant marriage came to its issue. Men were facing the danger either of not developing the Ego by remaining within the separate racial stocks, or of losing all connection with humanity as such and becoming independent, self-sufficient, egoistic individuals.

This decisive point had been reached. What must now happen? Something quite specific. The human Ego must become sufficiently mature to develop within itself what may for the first time properly be called *freedom*, and to unfold from within itself, in freedom, the love which, because it now belongs to the life of soul, is no longer bound up with the blood-tie. The Ego was facing this decisive issue: to meet it, it must be completely liberated, must acquire full consciousness of itself. Thus, with the exception of the oriental peoples, the whole of mankind belonging to the old world

45

was confronting a birth of the Ego through which this Ego could know the love that springs from its own inmost being. Out of freedom the Ego was to unfold love, and out of love, freedom. Only a being who develops an Ego of this nature is in the real sense *man*. For a being whose love is determined solely by ties of blood is coerced into love, and merely gives expression to what, at a lower level, happens in the animal kingdom. It was at this point of history of which we have just been speaking that full manhood became, for the first time, a possibility. At this point the influence which made man truly man was to stream over the earth.

And now let us recall what I have said many times: that man is a being ensheathed in three members: the physical body which he has in common with the minerals, the etheric body which he has in common with the plants, and the astral body which up to this point of time had been the seat of the kind of love he has in common with the animals. With his fully developed Ego man is the crown of earthly creation. All other beings of the earth have names that can be given them from outside; they are objective realities. The " Ego " has a name that can be given only by itself. In the Ego, the ' I ', the Godhead speaks; earthly conditions have no longer a voice. In the ' I ' the kingdom of the Spirit speaks; the Spirit from the heavens speaks when the ' I ' has become fully self-conscious.—It might be said that until that time there were three kingdoms—mineral, plant, animal—and a kingdom which had indeed risen to a higher level than these, but had not yet reached completion, had not yet been imbued with its full super-earthly reality of being. This kingdom exists by virtue of the fact that into an Egohood there enters that which is otherwise nowhere to be found on earth, namely, the spiritual world, the kingdom of heaven.—This kingdom is called in the Bible " the kingdom— or the kingdoms—of heaven ", or, more usually " the kingdom of God."

" The kingdom of heaven " is simply an altern- ative expression for " the kingdom of man." When we speak of mineral, plant and animal kingdoms we can add in the words of the Bible a fourth, " the kingdom of man." Men who at that time, with the insight acquired in the Mysteries, could look back into the whole course of human evolution, could speak as follows: " Look back to ancient times: humanity was then only in process of being led to the level of manhood, for the king- dom of heaven is to come to the earth."—So spoke the forerunner of Christ-Jesus, and Christ-Jesus Himself: " The kingdom of heaven is at hand ". In these words they indicated the essential quality of that time. It was the age when the birth of Christ-Jesus had to take place. He was to bring to mankind the forces through which the Ego would be able to unfold, and develop its own inherent nature.

The whole evolution of humanity thus divides itself into two main phases: the phase when the kingdom of heaven is not yet on the earth, and the phase when the kingdom of heaven, the kingdom of

47

man in its highest sense, is actually on the earth. The ancient Hebrew people was chosen to provide the bodily constitution, the bodily sheaths, which would so develop as to become fit to receive the bearer of this kingdom of heaven.

These are the secrets revealed when the historical aspect of events is studied in the light of the deepest meaning of the Gospel of St. Matthew. To the two streams which we have seen[9] were contributory to Christianity—the streams of Zarathustrianism and Buddhism—we must add a third, namely, the stream contributed by the ancient Hebrew people. We see how these great Leaders, Buddha and Zarathustra, desired to bring to mankind the offering of the streams of spiritual life inaugurated by them. But a temple had to be provided and this could be done only through the ancient Hebrew people, who produced the temple which was the physical body of Jesus. Into the temple the two streams of Zarathustra and Buddha could bring their offerings. The first offering was made by Zarathustra, in that he incarnated in this body; the later offering was made by the Buddha, in that he rayed forth his Nirmanakaya,[10] into the other Jesus.*— In this way the two streams flow into a unity.

I have only been able to-day to give you a slight sketch of these deeper secrets and I have had to express it in a somewhat dogmatic way. We must continue our study on some other occasion, in order that we may acquire a clearer picture of the mission of the ancient Hebrew people and of the

* See Appendix II, p. 75

48

emergence of Christ-Jesus from this people. Then will become manifest to us this unique event, that out of history itself, out of the historical flow of evolution, there evolved a Being of everlasting value, imperishable and eternal. So shall we gradually come to understand how, out of a transient world, that was able to spring which will endure for eternity.

# III

As a contribution to studies connected with the Gospel of St. Matthew, something was said in the last lecture about the mission of the ancient Hebrew people and how Christ-Jesus sprang from this people. In studying the Gospels our aim is to understand little by little how the different streams of spiritual life converged, in order, eventually, in the great Christian stream, to provide in common for the further evolution of the earth. All that could be done in a brief study was to indicate in merest outline the part played by the ancient Hebrew people in the general evolution of mankind. But it is not possible to understand the Gospel of St. Matthew unless we at least give some consideration to certain other aspects of this people.

For the sake of clarity, let us once more remind ourselves of the soul-nature of the Hebrews, upon which their whole mission was dependent. We have seen that their mission differed from that of the other pre-Christian peoples. To the latter, that which they had inherited of the ancient clairvoyance of mankind was still an essential factor. Evidence of this clairvoyant knowledge is to be found among all the peoples of antiquity. We may speak of it as a ' primeval wisdom.' It can be described more exactly in the following way.—In old Atlantis, vision of the spiritual world was still the common heritage of men. Although the higher experiences were accessible only to Initiates, every human being had, at the very least, a definite conception of the spiritual world, because in certain intermediary states of consciousness the men of that epoch were still able to see into the spiritual realm. But this faculty had to be replaced by one that to-day is uppermost in man, that of intellectual reasoning, comprehension of the outer world by means of the physical senses; in other words, experience of the outer physical world. This faculty developed slowly, and by degrees, in the course of the pre-Christian era. A considerable residue of the old clairvoyance still survived in the people of ancient India. The teaching imparted by the Holy Rishis was a primeval wisdom, inherited from the far past. So too, in the second Post-Atlantean epoch of culture, what was known to the pupils and followers of Zarathustra in ancient Persia was a legacy of this old clairvoyance. Chaldean astronomy, and also the knowledge possessed by the ancient Egyptians, were both permeated with the ancient wisdom. A science derived from the faculties typical of later Post-Atlantean humanity would have been entirely unintelligible to the Egyptians and the Chaldeans. No science, expressing itself in the form of concepts and ideas of a physical nature, existed in those days. There was no reflective thinking such as we know it to-day.

It is by no means unimportant to be clear in our minds about the difference between a genuine seer of our own time and a seer, let us say, of ancient Chaldea or ancient Egypt. There is a very marked difference. One who in the life and conditions natural in our time unfolds genuine seership, must bring to bear upon the revelations, inspirations and experiences coming to him from the spiritual world, the logical reason he is able to acquire here in the physical world, through the exercise of normal, earthly thinking. The experiences of a seer in modern times can never be completely intelligible if they are not received by a soul thoroughly schooled in logical, reasoned thinking. In the modern age these inspirations and revelations from the spiritual world demand that logical thinking shall be brought to bear upon them. A person who has such inspirations to-day, but lacks the will to unfold logical thinking, to develop his earthly faculties healthily and selflessly, can never achieve more than what is called ' visionary clairvoyance ', which remains obscure and incomprehensible, and is for this reason bound to be misleading. Only a soul possessed of the resolute will to exercise *reason* can provide the right conditions for inspirations from the spiritual world in the modern age. That is why in a spiritual movement such as ours the greatest possible importance must be attached to the fact that seership shall not be developed, nor the revelations from the spiritual world proclaimed, in an amateurish, unbalanced way. The aim for which we must work is that the soul itself shall bring something to meet the inspirations and revelations. The development of seership demands the effort

52

and exertion required in rational thinking. In our time the two cannot be separated.

For an Egyptian or Chaldean seer it was an entirely different matter. *Together with* the inspirations—which arrived by quite another path—came the principles of thinking; hence he needed no separate system of thinking. When he had undergone spiritual training the principles of thinking were given to him complete, along with the inspirations themselves. The organism of modern man is no longer suited for this, it has grown out of it; for humanity is always moving on.

Only by bearing this difference clearly in mind can we fully understand what is implied by saying that vestiges of the old clairvoyance still survived in pre-Christian times, with the one exception of the ancient Hebrew people. They were chosen from the first, in order to develop a . human organism possessing the faculty of comprehending the outer physical world according to number, measure and weight, so that by this means they might gradually rise from knowledge of the physical world to knowledge of the spiritual reality comprised in the concept of Jahve or Jehovah. The all-essential point here is that in Abraham there had been chosen a man possessing a brain so constituted as to enable him to become the progenitor of a whole people, who would inherit these qualities from him and transmit them to their descendants. Spiritual promptings must be received, not merely as arising from within man, but as a gift from without. All that was derived from Abraham came, primarily, not from within, but as a revelation from without. This is a factor of immense importance, radically distinguishing the character of this people from that of the other peoples of antiquity.

You can well imagine that the old inherited faculties could not disappear all at once, but that vestiges remained, even in this people. It was so in the case of Joseph who in this respect still had much in common with the other peoples. For this reason he could be the link between the ancient Hebrews and the Egyptians, who were the latest to remain in the spiritual stream of the pre-Christian peoples. The development of the new faculties was bound to be only very gradual.

Why was a people prepared in this definite way? Why had a people to be chosen for separation from all the other forms of pre-Christian spiritual life, and why had they to be endowed with faculties of a special kind? All this had to take place to make it possible for mankind to be prepared for that great point of time—already drawing near— when Christ-Jesus was on earth. It was the point of time when all the old clairvoyance, all the conditions determined and restricted by blood-relationship had lost their significance and when something new entered into the life of man, namely, the full activity of the *Ego*. Through the widespread intermingling of blood, conditions which in earlier times had great meaning and purpose, passed away, but in their place came the possibility of the full activity of the human Ego. Thus the true kingdom of mankind—the *Kingdom of Heaven*—was added to the other kingdoms.

Now, speaking generally, when anything is born, men are not immediately prone to recognise it as what it really is. They certainly do not immediately recognise happenings of the spiritual life. They are very ready to speak of prophets who will come in the future—this was quite usual in the times both preceding and following the birth of Christianity. In the 12th and 13th centuries there was a veritable mania for prophecy. Here, there and everywhere people came forward proclaiming the imminent return of Christ, pointing to the places where He would appear. In other times, too, isolated phenomena of the kind have occurred. There has been talk about one person or another being the new incarnation of Christ.—No words need be wasted on the subject of such prophecies because even when they are made they bear evidence in themselves of their own defect. One defect they all have: they speak of an event that is to come, but neglect so to prepare men's hearts and minds that they are capable of recognising and understanding it. The position of these people reminds one of the incident of the teacher which Hebbel gives in his diary.—The teacher gives a severe thrashing to a particular pupil because he cannot understand Plato. Hebbel adds, jokingly, that the pupil was the reincarnated Plato himself! This is the sort of thing that happens to people who are constantly talking about a Christ who is to come again. They would be little prepared for the reality, even were it to appear; they would take the Christ for something altogether different from the Christ.

Preparation for the Christ had therefore to be made in advance. This must be realised, before it is possible to understand the Gospel of St. Matthew. Preparation was necessary in order that there might at least be a few human beings capable of understanding the Christ Event, which—to characterise one aspect only—consisted in knowing that Christ was the One Who made it possible for men thenceforth to receive *from without*, not physical impressions only, but also the Spirit. For this, individual men had to be prepared.

In point of fact, right through Hebrew history, some individuals were, by certain methods, prepared to be able to understand the Christ Event. In the earliest times there were only a few of these men, but they and their way of life must be closely studied if we are to realise what careful preparations were made for the coming of Christ, how the Hebrew people, with the qualities they had inherited from Abraham, were rendered capable of a prophetic understanding of how the human Ego would be brought to man through the Saviour. Those men who were prepared so as to be able to recognise and understand, by *clairvoyance*, the significance of the Christ, were called Nazarenes.[11] These men were able to perceive *clairvoyantly* all that had been prepared from the earliest days of the Hebrews, in order that, out of and through this people, the Christ might be born and understood. In a mode of life compatible with the development of clairvoyant insight, these Nazarenes were bound by strict and strenuous rules. These rules, since they

56

belonged to quite another age, differ considerably from those essential for the attainment of spiritual knowledge to-day, although in some respects there is a certain similarity. Much that was of primary importance in the Nazarene training is subsidiary to-day, and much that was subsidiary then would now be essential. Nobody should imagine that methods which in earlier times led to clairvoyant knowledge of Christ would have the effect of leading a man of the modern age to the same momentous recognition.

The first demand made of a Nazarene was total abstention from all alcohol; indeed, the taking of any food prepared with vinegar was most strictly forbidden. Those who obeyed the prescribed rules to the letter were obliged to refrain from consuming anything whatsoever derived from the grape. This was because it was held that in the grape the plant-forming principle has overstepped a certain point, namely the point where the sun-forces alone are working on the plant. In the grape there are at work, not the sun-forces alone, but something that develops inwardly and has already matured by the time the sun-forces are weakening in the autumn. Hence anything deriving from the grape might be drunk only by those who did not aspire to the higher form of clairvoyance, but who worshipped the god Dionysos and were content that their faculties should rise up as it were out of the earth. Further, as long as his preparation and training lasted, the Nazarene was committed never to touch or come into contact with anything that has an astral body and can die; briefly, the Nazarene must avoid anything of an animal nature. In the strictest sense of the word he must be a vegetarian. Therefore in certain regions the strictest Nazarenes fed only on the carob bean, the so-called ' St. John's bread '; this was a very common food among them. They also fed on the honey of wild bees—not cultivated bees—and other honey-seeking insects. John the Baptist, in later days, adopted this way of life, feeding on the carob bean and wild honey. In the Gospels it is said that his food was locusts and wild honey, but this must be regarded as a mistranslation.—I have elsewhere called your attention to other mistranslations of the same kind.[12]

Another of the main stipulations in the preparation for seership was that during the period of their training the Nazarenes must not allow their hair to be cut. The reason for this is intimately connected with the whole process of human evolution. This relationship of hair to human evolution is a fundamental fact. All in man that concerns his true being can be understood only if we try to see it against its spiritual background. Strange as it may sound, in our hair we have a relic of certain rays by which the sun-forces were once instilled into man. What the sun in earlier times thus instilled into man was something *living*. We find clear illustrations of this in times when man still had consciousness of deeper realities. For example, in many ancient sculptures of lions it is clearly evident that the sculptuor's aim was not simply to copy a lion as we know it to-day with its mane. A sculptor, still cognisant of the traditions born of ancient knowledge, portrayed a lion in such a way as to convey the impression that the hairs in the mane seem to be inserted into the body as if from outside, like instreaming rays of the sun which have, as it were, hardened into hairs. One can therefore well imagine that in ancient time it might have been quite possible, by leaving the hair uncut, to receive certain forces into one's being, especially if the hair was young and healthy.—But even in the times of Hebrew antiquity this was, in point of fact, regarded among the Nazarenes as hardly more than a symbol.

The progress of mankind however, did in fact depend to some measure upon his allowing the spiritual reality behind the sun to stream into his being. The fact that as time went on man was born as a less and less hairy being was symptomatic of his advance from the old, upwelling gift of clairvoyance to reasoned thought concerning the outer world. We must picture the men of the Atlantean and earliest Post-Atlantean epochs with a copious growth of hair—a sign that spiritual light was still shining down upon them in great strength. As the Bible tells, the choice was made between the smooth-skinned Jacob and the hairy Esau. In Esau we must see a descendant of Abraham in whom the last residue of an ancient phase of human evolution still survived, manifesting in his growth of hair. The man possessed of faculties leading him outward into the world around, is represented in Jacob, who was gifted with the qualities of cleverness with all its darker sides. Esau is ousted by Jacob.

59

Thus in Esau another offshoot of the main line of development is cast aside. From him sprang the Edomites, in whom old, inherited faculties continued to be propagated.—All these things are accurately and beautifully expressed in the Bible.

But now there had to arise in man a new consciousness of the spiritual life, and it had to arise, in a new way, in the Nazarene, through keeping his hair uncut during the time of his preparation. The relation of hair to the light of the spirit in the ancient world is confirmed by the fact that with the exception of an insignificant cipher, " light " and " hair " are expressed in the ancient Hebrew language by the same word. The ancient Hebrew tongue is full of indications of the deepest secrets of human evolution and must be regarded as a momentous revelation of wisdom through language. Such, then, was the purpose underlying the Nazarene custom of allowing the hair to grow long.—To-day, of course, this is no longer essential.

During the time of his preparation the Nazarene had to be led to a very definite clairvoyant experience which would reveal to him that the approach of Christ to mankind was drawing near. The last great Nazarene lived at the time of Christ. His name was John the Baptist. Not only had he himself experienced the complete experience of the Nazarene training but he enabled all those whom he aspired to bring to their true manhood, to experience it likewise.[13] This complete experience is nothing else than the *Baptism of John*. It is important to understand exactly what its effect was upon their inner development. What was this Baptism, and to what did it lead? In the first place a man was plunged under water, the effect being that his etheric body in the region of his head was loosened somewhat from the physical body, whereas normally the etheric body is firmly knit with the physical body. It is well known that if a man is on the point of drowning, the whole tableau of his life flashes before him as a result of the loosening of his etheric body. This was what happened in the Baptism given by John. A man beheld his life-tableau, events of his life otherwise completely forgotton. Moreover the nature and constitution of the human in that particular epoch was also revealed to him. The physical body evolves out of the shaping and moulding which it receives from the etheric body, but this member of man's being which gives form to the physical body can be perceived only if it is loosened from the physical body, as happened in the Baptism of John.

If a man had undergone such a baptism three thousand years before our era, he would have become conscious that the highest spiritual condition that can be bestowed upon the human being can only come to him as a heritage from the ancient past—for whatever was given to man out of the spiritual worlds in very ancient times was essentially a heritage. This heritage of the past was portrayed in the etheric body and acted as a formative force upon the physical body. Even to those who had developed beyond the normal stage, such a baptism would have revealed that all their knowledge was founded upon ancient spirit-inspiration. This experience was described as the vision of the soul-nature of the etheric body, in the form of the Serpent. Those who had had this experience were called *Children of the Serpent*, because they had seen how the Luciferic beings had descended into the being of man; how the etheric body which had given the physical body its form and shape was itself a creation of the Serpent.

Now, however, in a baptism, not three thousand years before John the Baptist, but in his own day, something quite different came to light. Among those who were baptised there were some whose very nature gave evidence of the progress in human evolution: namely, of the vastly increased power of the Ego, derived from its experience of the outer visible world. Moreover the picture arising for them was entirely different from that revealed at the earlier baptisms. Men now beheld the creative forces of the etheric body, no longer in the image of the Serpent, but in the image of the *Lamb*.* This etheric body was no longer permeated from within by what issued from the Luciferic forces, but was wholly surrendered to the spiritual world which shines into the souls of men *through the phenomena of the outer world*. In the Baptism of John this vision of the Lamb came to those who were able to understand what at that time Baptism signified. Moreover they knew from what they themselves experienced, that man had become an altogether different, a quite new being. The few who experi-

*See Appendix III, p. 76

enced this at the Baptism of John were able to say:
A great and momentous event has come to pass;
man has become a different being; the Ego has now
the rulership on earth!—Among those whom John
baptised there were some who had been made ready
to understand the signs of the times, to recognise
that so supreme an event had come to pass.[14]

This had always been the goal of the Nazarenes.
Through the experience brought by this Baptism
they recognised that the coming of Christ was near
at hand. This they knew from the form in which the
etheric body appeared before them, when loosened
in the baptism. It was the mission of John the
Baptist to reveal that now the time had come when
the Ego could express itself fully in man's nature;
thereby he brought the ages of antiquity to their
fulfilment. He gathered around him a community
to whom he was able to reveal that now, through
the emergence of the Ego in the real sense, the
Christ Principle could draw into mankind. John
the Baptist brought the Nazarene movement to such
a height, that, out of his prophecy alone, it found
its fulfilment. He gathered around him a community able to understand the approaching Christ
Event.—Only in this light are the words spoken
by John the Baptist intelligible. Such words must
be taken in their deepest meaning. It is quite
wrong that students of these matters to-day should
regard John the Baptist merely as a raging fanatic,
a man who storms at the Pharisees, calling them
" a generation of vipers ", and cries out to them:
" Think not to say within yourselves, We have

63

Abraham to our father; for I say unto you, that God is able of these stones to raise up children unto Abraham." (St. Matt. III, 9).—John the Baptist would have been no more than a brawler, had he not rejoiced when Pharisees and Sadducees came to him to be baptized. Nevertheless when they come, he inveighs against them. Why is this?

When the inner meaning of these things is understood it is at once obvious that the words are not just outpourings of fanatical abuse, but have profound significance. This, however, can only be understood by reflecting upon a certain feature in the history of the ancient Hebrew people.

From what has been said it will be clear to you that in Abraham there had been chosen a man whose constitution was such that at the right time the Christ could be born of his descendants. But this required the development and elaboration of faculties which had been present in Abraham as rudiments only. We must realise that if these rudiments were to be unfolded it was constantly necessary for certain elements to be eliminated. We have already seen how this happened in the case of Joseph, but there were even earlier examples, such as Esau, from whom the Edomites descended, because in him too an ancient heritage had remained. Only such qualities as were compatible with the goal described were to be preserved. This is indicated in a wonderful way.—Abraham had two sons: Isaac, the son of Sarah, and Ishmael. The Hebrew nation were the descendants of Isaac. In Abraham, however, there were other qualities as well. If these other

64

qualities had been transmitted through the Hebrew generations, the right conditions would not have been achieved. Hence this different element must be radically thrust away into another line of descendants, into the descendants of Ishmael, the son of Hagar, the Egyptian bond-woman. Therefore two lines of descent go out from Abraham, the one through Isaac, and the other through the outcast Ishmael, who having the blood of an Egyptian in his veins, must have in his constitution elements unfitting for the mission of the Hebrew people.

But now something momentous comes to pass! The task of the Hebrew people was to propagate in the direct line of heredity the qualities that were intrinsically their own, and everything that was an ancient heritage, ancient wisdom, had to be imparted to them from *without*. Hence they had to go to Egypt in order to receive what could be given to them there. Moses was able to impart this to his people because he was an Egyptian initiate. But he certainly could not have done so had he possessed wisdom merely in its Egyptian form. It would be erroneous to imagine that the ancient Egyptian wisdom could be simply grafted on to what flowed down from Abraham. This would not have been compatible with the intrinsic character of the Hebrew people and would have produced an abortive form of culture. Moses brought with him to the wisdom he acquired from his Egyptian initiation something of a quite different nature. Hence he could not simply impart to the Israelites what came from the Egyptian initiation. His first real gift to them was made after the revelation on Sinai, and made outside Egypt.

What, then, is the revelation on Sinai? What was vouchsafed to Moses there, and what was it that he imparted to the Israelites? He imparted something that could well be grafted into the stem of this people because it was related to them in a very definite way. In times past the descendants of Ishmael had wandered away from their country and had settled in the regions now traversed by Moses and his people. Moses found in the Ishmaelites, among whom there was Initiation of a certain kind, those attributes and qualities which had been transmitted to them through Hagar, qualities which were derived from Abraham, but in which were preserved many elements inherited from the ancient past. Out of the revelations that he received from this branch of the Hebrew people, it became possible for Moses to make the revelation of Sinai intelligible to the Israelites. In regard to this there is an ancient Hebrew legend that in Ishmael a shoot of Abraham was cast out into Arabia, that is, into the desert. What sprang from this stock is contained in the teaching of Moses. On Sinai, the ancient Hebrew people received back again, in the Mosaic Law, what had been cast out from their blood: they received it back *from without*.

Here we also see how in the wonderful mission of the Hebrew people everything had to be *given to them;* had to be received back at a later stage as a gift. As a gift from without Abraham had, in Isaac, received the whole Hebrew nation. Again,

66

Moses and his people received back from the descendants of Ishmael what had once been thrust out from their midst. During the period of their isolation in the wilderness they had to build up their own constitution, and also receive back as a gift from their God, what they had cast out. So, too, Jacob was in the end reconciled with Esau, thus receiving again what, in Esau, had been cast away.—The Bible must be read with scrupulous attention if the import of the words it contains is to be rightly understood.

The whole history of the Hebrew people is full of significant happenings such as these. The *giving of the Law* by Moses is connected with something that springs from the descendants of Hagar, whereas the Hebrew *blood*, which represents the specific Israelitish faculties, springs from Sarah. Hagar or Agar in Hebrew is the same as *Sinai*, which means the ' stone mountain ', the great stone. One might say that Moses received the revelation of the Law from the ' great stone '—a material representation of Hagar. The Law given to this Judaic people did not spring from the highest faculties in Abraham, but from Hagar, from Sinai. Those, therefore, who are followers merely of the Law as given on Sinai—that is, the Pharisees and the Sadducees—are exposed to the danger of their development coming to a standstill. They are those who at the Baptism of John will see, not the *Lamb*, but the *Serpent*.

Viewed in this light, what would otherwise seem to be mere abuse on the part of the Baptist becomes

67

a righteous warning to the Pharisees and Sadducees
when he cries out to them: ' Ye who are followers
of the Serpent, take heed that in the baptism ye have
the true vision '; —that is to say, the vision of the
Lamb, not of the Serpent!  He also tells them that
they must not rely upon the fact that they have
Abraham as their father.  For this came to their
lips as a mere phrase; they were swearing by what
had proceeded from the Sinai stone, but had now
ceased to have significance.  ' Now'—said the
Baptist—' out of the universe there is drawing near
the newborn Ego, and this Ego I make known to
you.  I declare to you how out of Judaism there
will spring the true inheritance which has been
carried down the generations, and to which men will
swear allegiance, not now by the stone of Sinai,
but by that which is everywhere round about us.
The children of God will be made manifest, when,
behind the material, the spiritual will be visible.
Out of these stones God's word is able to raise up
children unto Abraham.  You speak without
understanding when you say: ' We have Abraham
as our father '.

Only in the light of what has here been said is
meaning imparted to these words of the Baptist.
Nor are such things disclosed by the Akasha
Chronicle alone; they stand in the Bible itself.
Compare the words of the Apostle Paul in his
Epistle to the Galatians (IV, 24, 25).  What I have
told you here is confirmed by St. Paul.  He too says
that the word Hagar or Agar is identical with Sinai
and indicates that what was given on Sinai is a

68

covenant which must be outgrown by those who, through the development of the essential qualities of Abraham in the successive generations, are now to realise what has come into the world through Christ.

This again points to a saying which must in future be understood. It is pitiful indeed that in an age when intelligence has reached such heights, men have yet given so little reflection to such words as: "Repent ye!" According to the real meaning, the translation should be somewhat as follows: 'Change the tenor of your minds!' In many passages it is said that John baptised unto repentance, that is to say, he baptized with water *in order that* a change might take place in the tenor and attitude of the soul. When those who had been baptized came out of the water, it behoved them so to change the tenor of their souls that they no longer looked back to the old traditions, but forward to what the freed Ego, which Christ would give, should contain. The hearts and minds of men were to be turned from the direction leading to the ancient gods into the direction leading to the new divine-spiritual Beings. It was in this sense that the Baptism of John was to bring about a change of heart and soul. John baptized with water in order that there might be called forth in some human beings the power to recognise the coming of the Kingdom of Heaven, and with that recognition to understand who Christ-Jesus is.

Herewith something more has been added to what we have already come to know of the mission of the ancient Hebrew people. All these things will lead step by step to a better understanding of Christ. We have seen how the mission of the Hebrews takes shape with most wonderful inner coherence. We have seen how there were present in Abraham, faculties which developed in the Hebrew people through successive generations. This required that many elements should be discarded and that the suitable elements should develop further in the blood, through propagation. That for which this people from Abraham onwards were specially gifted and chosen, was concentrated in one single Being, in Jesus. The Jews had to be maintained in their mission by a teaching; but that teaching had to come from without, and, in point of fact, from what they themselves had once cast out. The elements derived from Ishmael might not remain in the *blood*, but must be present purely in the domain of *knowledge*. This the Hebrew people received back again in the giving of the Law by Moses on Sinai. This Law had fulfilled its purpose at the point of time when what had come from the " stone " was no longer needed, but when men possessed what was to be bestowed upon mankind from the universe. Thus slowly and gradually preparation was made for the time when out of the stones, the sons of God—that is, the race of Man—could arise, when, behind all ' stones ', behind all the earth, the spiritual world should be made manifest.

These are but fragmentary contributions towards an understanding of the mission of the Hebrew people. Only when we fully understand this mission can we begin to comprehend the majestic figure of Christ-Jesus as presented to us in the Gospel of St. Matthew.

## Appendix I (p. 28)

The great truth that in Abraham there began a new relationship of mankind to the material and spiritual worlds is a main theme of these three lectures, and it is worth while considering it in the light of the evolution of human consciousness which Rudolf Steiner revealed as the clue to the understanding of human history. In the ancient Indian civilisation man, in his consciousness, was still a dweller in the spiritual world, and the material world was "Maya", Illusion, a world in which he did not feel at home and from which he longed to escape.

In the ancient Persian civilisation it was revealed to man that the material world was itself a manifestation of spirit, and the scene of a great spiritual conflict of Light against Darkness, in which man had a part to play, Man's powers of perception were still predominantly supersensible.

In the Chaldean-Egyptian civilisation man became more and more absorbed in his experience of the physical world through his senses, and his powers of spiritual perception diminished. Two dangers threatened him. First, that he should regard the objects of the outer world merely as affording him the means for a variety of experiences, in which his unbridled passions and lust for power would have free play; secondly, that, being no longer able to

72

perceive spiritual beings behind natural phenomena, he should make gods out of the phenomena themselves. This would lead to idolatry. These two trends were manifest in the Babylonian world into which Abraham was born. They were bound to lead man further and further from his spiritual destiny.

While he still retained clairvoyant powers, man's etheric body, which was the instrument of spiritual perception, was not wholly contained within the confines of the physical body. With Abraham the withdrawal of the etheric body into the physical body was more advanced, and the etheric forces, which had formerly exercised perception independently of the body, withdrew within the skull—the " cave " in which it was said Abraham was born—and functioned as *Thought*, playing upon the experiences of the physical world which were conveyed through the portals of the sense-organs. This Thought-activity upon sense-experience began to reveal the multiple relationships of " measure, weight and number " by which the diversity of sense-phenomena were brought into unity, and to discover behind this the being and working of Jehovah.

This attitude to the phenomena of Nature—never as being in themselves a manifestation of the Divine, but always as a revelation of Divine wisdom and power—is peculiar to the Hebrew race. It finds expression frequently in the Psalms. " The heavens declare the glory of God; and the firmament showeth his handiwork." " The voice of the Lord is mighty in operation; the voice of the Lord is a glorious voice." " O Lord, how manifold are thy works;

73

in wisdom hast thou made them all. The earth is full of thy riches; so is the great and wide sea also." So too, when the Lord confounds both Job and his friends, it is by his wisdom and power manifest in the created world.

This special relationship of number and weight is summed up in Isaiah in one verse (XL, 12): " Who hath measured the waters in the hollow of his hand, and meted out heaven with the span, and comprehended the dust of the earth in a measure, and weighed the mountains in scales, and the hills in a balance?"

The same thought is expressed by Jesus in his teaching in the New Testament. " Not a sparrow falls to the ground without your heavenly Father." " The very hairs of your head are numbered."

Thus, man's growing awareness of the physical world, which, in the case of other nations, finally hid the divine and spiritual from him, led the Hebrews to perceive God behind, yet separate from, material objects, and so also behind all human life, and in a special way related to themselves. The psycho-physical organism of thought, which made this possible, originated in Abraham, and was passed down through their generations by a strictly-guarded heredity.

This special quality in Abraham is treated at greater length by Rudolf Steiner in the third lecture of the Course on *The Gospel of St. Matthew*, and also by Dr. Emil Bock in his *Primeval History*, chapter 3. It is also referred to by Philo of Alexandria in his allegorical study of Abraham.

74

*Note on two Jesus Children*

Rudolf Steiner explained the great difficulty of reconciling the Incarnation accounts in St. Matthew and St. Luke, by revealing that they each refer to a separate Jesus-child, born, as the Gospels assert, from different Davidic lines. How these children grew up together, and how their beings were finally united as the being of Jesus of Nazareth, is related by Dr. Steiner in the lecture-courses entitled *The Gospel of St. Luke*, *The Gospel of St. Matthew*, *From Jesus to Christ*, and others. It is a mystery which it is impossible to treat adequately in a note. These present lectures, however, show us the detailed, age-long provision by the spiritual powers, of the physical organism which could be the vehicle of the incarnating Christ. While they treat mostly of the purely physical preparation through the Hebrew race, they also speak of the spiritual inheritance through Zarathustra, and the soul-bestowal of Buddha. It is the harmonising of these three " sheaths " of past inheritance in one being that is explained by the revelation of the fact of these two children, a mystery of which there are only a few uncomprehended traces in the Gospels. It is a mystery of great importance, which can only be apprehended by patient, unprejudiced study.

75

## Appendix III

### The Serpent and the Lamb (see p. 62)

What Dr. Steiner is giving here is of the greatest importance and must be clearly understood.

What was given in the Baptism experience was a vision of the etheric body. To the baptized this was a revelation of his connection with the spiritual world, and of his being as the result of his whole past. In this he saw how his etheric body—and consequently its effect upon his physical body—had been deeply influenced by the Luciferic beings who had united themselves with it.

He saw his etheric body in the form of the SERPENT. Dr. Steiner does not here enlarge upon this image, though he speaks of it elsewhere. It would appear in two ways to be a significant image. The serpent exists in almost undifferentiated length. Moreover, as it grows it sloughs its skin, and emerges whole, a complete image of its former being, upon which there hardens the new and larger skin, and so on. It is an earthly image of man's reincarnations, sloughing off the physical body, but keeping the whole impress of the inner experience of the bodily existence, upon and out of which is fashioned a new body. The temptation of Eve was to seek satisfaction in her experience of the outer world. The tempter was the SERPENT.

76

In John's Baptism the etheric body was to be seen under the image of the LAMB. What did that signify?

The fundamental feature of the etheric world is the interrelationship of all its parts, and the capacity of the soul to experience itself in other souls and to receive them into its own experience. This is the etheric expression of man's true spiritual nature. In the physical world, it is realised in sacrifice and self-offering, of which the Lamb is the symbol. Man was to see the outer physical world, not merely as the stage of his own inner experience, but as the place where he was to learn obedience to the laws of his own spiritual being. He was to identify his newly-evolving ego, which no longer only discovered itself in the etheric manifestation of its inner experience, but was seeking to realise itself in the physical body, in mastery over the outer world,—he was to identify it with the Lamb: the outer world was to be to him a path of self-offering and sacrifice. Thus the new etheric body was to bear the image of the LAMB, and was to imprint that image upon man's physical body in which the ego was manifesting itself. In this, man would be opposed by the self-centredness of Lucifer.

This formation of the etheric body as the Lamb could not arise out of man's old serpent-like etheric body. It was to be the gift of Christ, who would thereby triumph over Lucifer. This would be manifest in Jesus.

Could it have been manifest in some incipient form in some of those baptized by John? Yes, in

77

some, specially prepared. The Nazarenes—the Essenes—manifested this self-offering life. They were universally regarded as manifesting the purest, most unselfish communal life. They would be forerunner souls, fitted from their past to have the change wrought by Christ in their etheric body, so as to fit them for the change in their physical being when He came to the earth. Some who were baptized by John could not have this experience, namely, the Pharisees, the " children of the Serpent." To others he could say, without explanation, " Behold!  The Lamb of God! "

[1] The lecture-courses here referred to are the following:

p.9 *The Gospel of St. John. 12 lectures. Hamburg, May, 1908. The Gospel of St. John and its Relation to the other Gospels. 14 lectures.* Cassel, June/July, 1909.

*The Gospel of St. Luke.* 10 lectures. Basle, September, 1909

[2] Lectures on the *Background to the Gospel of St. Mark* were

p.17 given in Berlin, October, 1910. The course of 14 lectures entitled *The Gospel of St. Mark,* was given in Berlin, September, 1912.

[3] These are the recognised names in spiritual science for the earlier

p.26 planetary conditions of the Earth. See *Occult Science: An Outline.*

[4] "Discursive thinking" would be an alternative translation of *das*

p.27 *urteilende Denken,* the expression used by Rudolf Steiner here. "Discursive as opposed to intuitive cognition, is attained by a series of inferences rather than by direct insight." (Runes: *Dictionary of Philosophy,* 4th ed. New York, 1942).

[5] This point, that the Hebrew heritage was not a matter merely of

p.32 natural descent, but of divine choice and gift, is developed by St. Paul from a somewhat different view-point in Romans IX, 8. "It is not the children of the flesh (Ishmael) that are children of God, but the children of the promise (Isaac) are reckoned for a seed." Cp. also Romans IV, 13–21.

[6] Genesis XXII, 17.

p.33

[7] In his book *Knowledge of the Higher Worlds: How is it*

p.34 *Achieved?* Rudolf Steiner speaks of the "lotus-flowers" as organs in the astral body connected with the development of supersensible perception. He points out that the name "lotus-flower" is only a traditional metaphorical designation. These organs are also known in technical esoteric language as "wheels" or "chakrams."

[8] This role of Moses is indicated in his traditional representation

p.37 as having two ram's horns springing from his forehead.

[9] See Rudolf Steiner's lecture-course: *The Gospel of St. Luke.*

p.48

[10] The spiritual reality resulting from his earthly existence.

p.48

79

[11] According to Biblical commentaries, *Nazarene* means
*p.56* ' branch ', or ' separated one ".   In lecture VI of the Course
entitled *The Gospel of St. Matthew*, Rudolf Steiner refers to
a community of the Essene sect connected particularly with
Netzer, a pupil of Jeshu ben Pandira, in Nazareth, or Netzereth.

[12] Locust—the fruit of the carob-tree; a locust-bean.
*p.58* The Greek name ἀκείς, properly denoting the insect, is applied
in the Levant to the carob-pod, from some resemblance in
form: and from very early times it has been believed by many
that the " locusts " eaten by John the Baptist were these pods.
*Oxford English Dictionary*.

[13] This statement is corroborated by a passage in Origen's
*p.60* work, *Concerning Prayer*. " John the Baptist knew certain secret
teaching about prayer, which he imparted, probably not to
all who were being baptized, but to those who were being
instructed in the secret doctrine as a preparation for baptism."
This throws light on the words of the disciples to Christ:
" Lord teach us to pray, even as John also taught his disciples."
(St. Luke XI, 1).   Rudolf Steiner's statement that John had
instructed his disciples about the Lamb also throws light upon
the seemingly abrupt announcement by John the Baptist to
his disciples, " Behold the Lamb of God." (St. John I, 29).

[14] Cp. Romans, VIII, 19.   " The earnest expectation of the
*p.63* created world waiteth for the manifestation of the sons of
God."


## *Note by Publisher*

Catalogues of all the published works of Rudolf Steiner in
print, in English translation, also the works of other authors on
Anthroposophy, can be obtained from:

Rufolf Steiner Press and Bookshop,          Rudolf Steiner Bookshop,
38, Museum Street,                                35, Park Road,
London WC1A 1LP                              London NW1 6XT